MAP READERS

Heinemann Library
Chicago, Illinois

Mapping Your Way

Ana Deboo

© 2007 Heinemann Library
a division of Reed Elsevier Inc.
Chicago, Illinois

Customer Service 888-454-2279

Visit our website at www.heinemannlibrary.com

Designed by David Poole and Geoff Ward
Illustrations by International Mapping (www.internationalmapping.com)
Photo research by Alan Gottlieb and Tracy Cummins
Originated by Modern Age
Printed and bound in China by WKT

08 07 06
10 9 8 7 6 5 4 3 2 1

Library of Congress Cataloging-in-Publication Data
Deboo, Ana.
  Mapping your way / Ana Deboo.-- 1st ed.
      p. cm. -- (Map readers)
  Includes bibliographical references and index.
  ISBN 1-4034-6790-0 (hc) -- ISBN 1-4034-6797-8 (pb)
  1. Map reading--Juvenile literature. I. Title. II. Series.
  GA130.D346 2007
  912--dc22

                                     2006003370

Acknowledgments
The author and publisher are grateful to the following for permission to reproduce copyright material
Courtesy American Museum of Natural History p. **23**; Corbis pp. **5**, **19**, **27** (Tony West), **29**; MapPoster.com pp. **4**, **22**; MapQuest, Inc. p. **26**; National Park Service p. **24**; 2005 New York-New Jersey Trail Conference, Inc.; www.nynjtc.org. Used by permission pp. **5**, **25**; Perry-Castaneda Library Map Collection/University of Texas at Austin p. **13**; Universal Map pp. **7**, **11**, **14**, **16**, **17**, **18**; Washington Metropolitan Area Transit Authority (WMATA) p. **20**.

The map on page 15 appears courtesy of Adventure Cycling Association: Adv-cycling.org.

Cover image reproduced with permission of Universal Map.
Cover photo of compass with permission of Silvia Bukovacc/Shutterstock.

Special thanks to Daniel Block for his help in the production of this book.

Table of Contents

Introduction 4

Finding Your Way Around a Map 6

Road Maps 12

City and Town Maps 18

Neighborhood and Other Limited-Area Maps 22

Other Maps That Help You Find Your Way 24

Maps of the Future 26

Map Activity: Find Your Way in the Capital City 28

Glossary 30

Further Reading 31

Index 32

Some words are shown in bold, **like this**. You can find out what they mean by looking in the glossary.

Introduction

Maybe you have had an experience like this: You and your mom are on the way to a party in the next town. Suddenly Mom, who is driving the car, says, "This doesn't look familiar. Where *are* we?" She pulls over into a nearby parking lot and stops the car. From the back seat, you can hear paper rattling as she unfolds a map. She might mutter a bit, saying things like, "Hmm. Did we already pass Alder Street?" But pretty soon, she figures out exactly where you are. Using the map, she finds her way to the party.

Maps are pictures of places, specially designed to tell you where things are, and they come in many types. Some show the whole world, but most focus on smaller parts of it—continents, countries, states, cities, and neighborhoods. They can tell you the name and location of a place. They can show you natural features such as oceans, lakes, rivers, and mountains. Or they might show the location of manmade landmarks like campgrounds, churches, schools, and monuments. Some maps show the lumps and bumps of the land: these are called topographic maps. Others give information about the places shown on them. For example, a map that shows how many people live in the different cities in a state is called a population density map. A map that shows what kinds of crops are grown in different parts of the state is a type of agricultural map.

Tourist picture map.

Probably the most common reason for using a map is to answer that familiar question: "Where *are* we?" This book will tell you how to choose the right map and use it to find your way. If you are going to take a long-distance driving trip, you probably need a road or highway map. Once you arrive at your destination, you will want to look at a town or city map. And if you are exploring a neighborhood, there is a map for that, too.

You will also learn about other common maps that help you get places, like the maps you need when you go hiking, the ones you see in public places like zoos, and the maps you will find when you plan a trip on a bus or on the subway.

The more familiar you are with these maps, the more places you will be able to explore. Who knows when you might find yourself on the move in an unfamiliar place? A map will rescue you every time.

Hiking trail map.

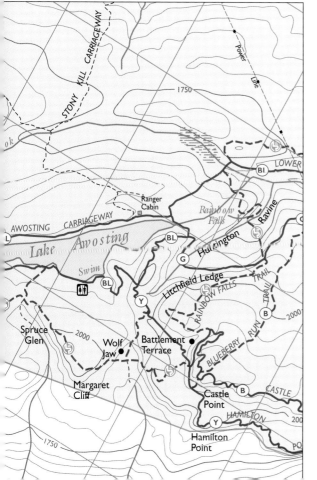

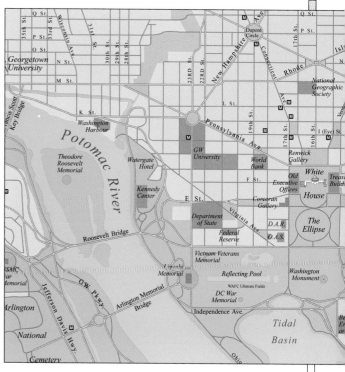

City map.

Maps can show many different types of information. These are some of the maps you will learn about in this book.

Finding Your Way Around a Map

There are many types of maps, and they all pack a lot of information into limited space. So **cartographers** (mapmakers) have created a few basic tools to help readers understand what they are looking at. If you learn how to use these tools, you will be ready to find your way using almost any map.

Start by looking at the **map title**. Books and songs sometimes have titles that do not really give you an idea of what they are about, but a map's title will always tell you what place is being described. It may also say what kind of a map it is.

The next thing to look at is the **map scale**. Maps are pictures of places drawn from the point of view of somebody floating in the air above and looking down at them. Let's say you took a sheet of paper up to the top of a skyscraper. From there you could draw a map that showed a few city blocks. If you were flying in a helicopter instead, you would be even higher up, so you could show more of the city on the paper. If you were in an airplane, you could probably draw the whole city. And if you were in a spaceship, you could draw a map of the entire Earth. The farther away your point of view, the more you can fit onto that same sheet of paper.

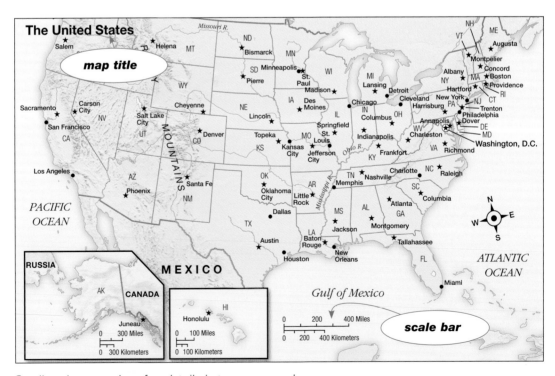

Small-scale maps show few details but can cover a large area.

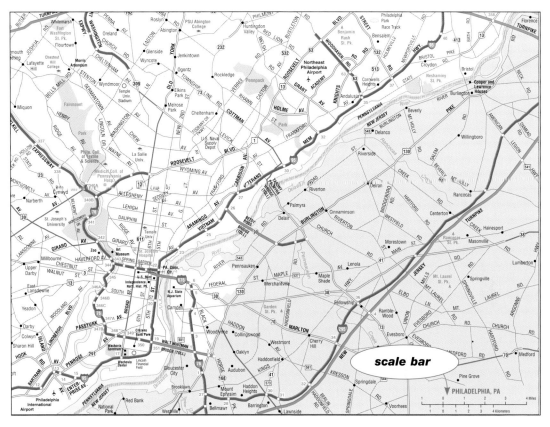

Large-scale maps show a small area in great detail.

A map's **scale bar** shows how much smaller the area on the map is compared to real life. The scale bar is a line with tick marks and numbers like a ruler. It is usually found on a bottom corner of the map. It tells you how many miles on the land are represented by each inch on the paper (or each centimeter, if the mapmaker uses the metric system). There may also be a sentence that says the same thing in words—for example, "One inch equals twenty miles."

Maps that cover a large area—like world, country, or state maps—are called **small-scale maps**. You can remember this by thinking about how each detail on the map has to be tiny in order to fit. A map that shows a smaller area from close up—such as a neighborhood or town map—is called a **large-scale map**. Each detail on the map can be pretty large compared to maps that cover more ground.

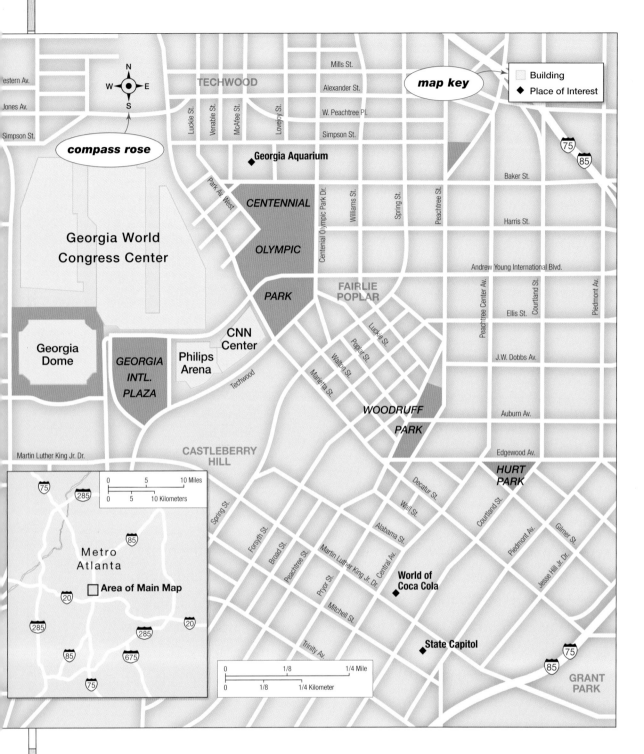

Once you have the right map, you are ready to get moving. Most maps have north at the top. North is one of the four **cardinal directions**, or points of the compass. The other three directions are south, east, and west. North points up toward the North Pole. South points the opposite direction, toward the South Pole. On a map, east points straight out to the right, and west points to the left. To confirm the directions on the map, look for the **compass rose**—a little picture showing the cardinal directions.

There are lots of labels on a map that give the names of cities, states, rivers, and more. But you will also see symbols, lines, and patches of different colors. Each of these gives useful information. Their meaning might be obvious. For example, a tiny airplane usually stands for an airport. Blue usually indicates a body of water such as a river, lake, or ocean. But sometimes the meaning of the symbol might be less clear. On road maps, different types of roads, such as freeways, scenic routes, and unpaved roads are indicated by lines of different thicknesses and colors. Colored patches indicate places that cover lots of ground, such as parks and urban areas. To find out what the symbols mean, look for the **map key**, also called the map legend.

For a collection of maps, such as a road atlas, a large map key may appear at the beginning of the book. It will not appear on the maps themselves.

ROADS, BOUNDARIES

EXIT NUMBER 405 — CONTROLLED ACCESS / INTERCHANGE		MILEAGE NUMBER / MILEAGE MARKER 6 — PRIMARY UNDIVIDED		- - - - - - - - TIME ZONE	
— TOLL CONTROLLED ACCESS		— ARTERIAL UNDIVIDED		- - - - - - - - TRAIL	
— PRIMARY DIVIDED		— STREET MINOR		— - — - — - - COUNTY BOUNDARY	
■ ■ ■ ■ ■ ■ UNDER CONSTRUCTION		- - - - - - - - - UNPAVED		STATE BOUNDARY	
— ARTERIAL DIVIDED		· · · · · · · · · · · · SCENIC ROUTE		INT'L BOUNDARY	

HIGHWAY SYMBOLS

INTERSTATE SHIELDS	U.S. HWY SHIELD	STATE HWY SHIELD	COUNTY HWY SHIELD	INDIAN HWY SHIELD	FOREST HWY SHIELD	AUTOROUTE SHIELD
⬟ ⬟ ⬟ BUS	{101} {41}	(299) (60)	550 39	5	5	5

SYMBOLS & FRILLS

▲ STATE/LOCAL PARK	✈ COMMERCIAL AIRPORT	▲▲ REST AREAS	⬗ CUSTOM STATION
▲ FOREST	■ POINT OF INTEREST	ⓘ INFORMATION CTR	✪ STATE CAPITAL
☂ WILDLIFE REFUGE	+ PHYSICAL FEATURE Mt. Olympus	⚶ SKI AREA	◉ COUNTY SEAT
▲ CAMPGROUND		)(MOUNTAIN PASS	• CITY, TOWN

Cartographers use a system called the **geographic grid** to pinpoint places on Earth. This grid system uses imaginary lines, called **latitude** and **longitude** lines, that are always in the same places. Latitude lines run horizontally around the globe; they are also called parallels because latitudes do not ever meet. Longitude lines, called meridians, run vertically around the globe. Unlike latitude lines, they do cross—at the North Pole and South Pole.

Latitude lines tell how far north or south places are from the equator. This is a line halfway between the North Pole and South Pole. Longitude lines tell how far east or west they are from a longitude called the Prime Meridian, which passes through Greenwich, a borough of London, England. The locations are expressed in units called **degrees**, which measure circular shapes like the Earth. (There is a different kind of unit also called a degree that measures temperature.)

The blue lines on this map show the latitude and longitude lines. Look to the bottom of the map and the sides to find the degrees.

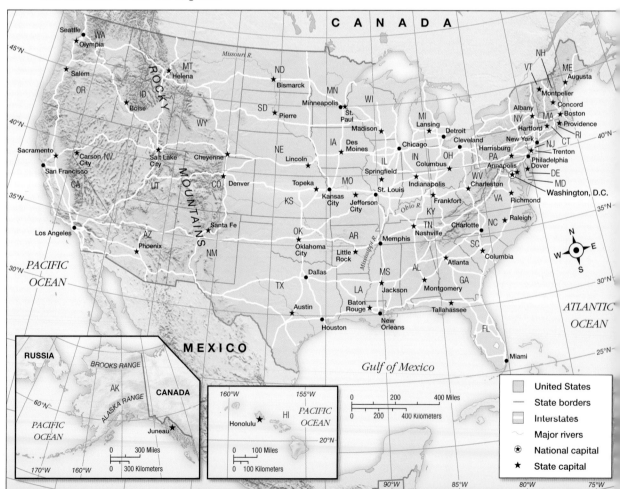

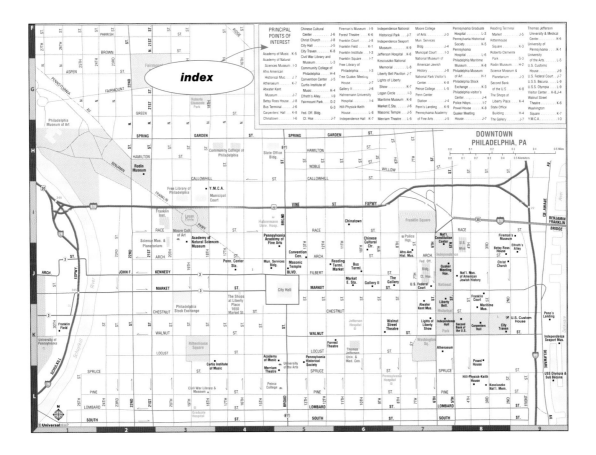

If you are using a map to find your way to a new place, you will use a different type of grid system. This type of grid is made up of thin vertical and horizontal lines that divide the map into squares. Usually, each column of squares has a letter, and each row has a number, or vice versa. Sometimes rows and columns are both numbered. Each square is identified by a letter-and-number pair. For example, the square in the third column, fourth row would be C4.

Maps that help you find your way around a location usually include an **index**. This is a list of places and their location on the map. A map index is a lot like a book index. If the index says a place is in J12, you can put your right index finger at the top of the J column and your left index finger at the beginning of the 12th row. Then move your fingers along the lines until they meet. You will find the location in that square.

Road Maps

Suppose you are going on a long trip in a car—across a whole state, for example. You will need a small-scale map of the state that shows the roads going from one place to another. This is called a road map, and it is one of the most common maps people use.

Road maps generally come in two forms: folded maps and atlases. A folded road map focuses on a specific area, often one state, but sometimes it shows two small states, such as Vermont and New Hampshire, or a region, such as New England. A road atlas is a book that contains a collection of road maps. Many road atlases with maps of all 50 states are available; you might want one of those if you are planning to drive across the country or across several states.

In addition to roads, road maps show basic information such as borders between states, the names of cities, states, and counties, and natural features like rivers, lakes, and mountains. Road maps show details of interest to tourists who are exploring the area. Airports, campgrounds, historic sites, and ferry routes across bodies of water are among the many things you will find. The symbols used are different from map to map. Be sure to consult the map key to figure out what they mean.

Early U.S. Road Maps

In the United States, road maps first became popular with the rise of bicycle clubs in the last part of the 1800s, and then truly grew with the rise of national highways. Many road maps were at first partially funded by automobile maker Carl Graham Fisher (1874–1939), who also founded the Indianapolis 500 car race. Towns would group together to promote a highway that connected them and put out maps of these highways and the attractions along them. Examples of this were the Lincoln Highway that ran from New York to San Francisco and the Dixie Highways that connected Chicago and Michigan to Miami. Later, companies that sold gas competed by giving customers road maps, and states promoted themselves through official state maps.

When planning a trip, it is a good idea to use a fairly new map because the condition of roads can change over time. For example, roads that are shown as unfinished on one map will be complete a few years later when a newer map is printed. The more up-to-date your map is, the less likely you are to encounter problems when traveling your planned route.

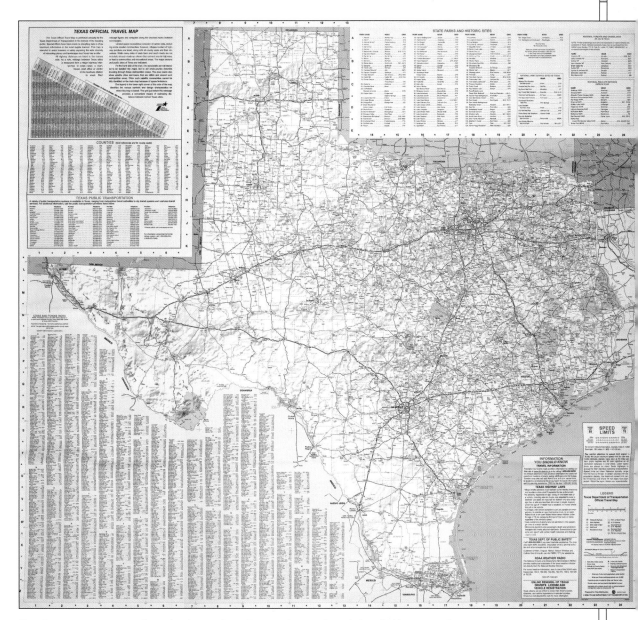

Road maps are generally quite large, but do not show a lot of detail. You may also need several large-scale maps to help you find your way in specific areas, such as towns you plan to visit.

A traveler planning a long trip is likely to have two main questions: "How far do I have to go?" and "What's the best way to get there?" A road map can answer both questions.

To help people who are traveling from one city to another over major roads, many maps include a **mileage table** (or mileage chart) that shows how long the journey is. This table has two lists of the city names on it, one arranged vertically along the left side and one horizontally across the top. To determine the distance—or **mileage**—between cities, find your departure city in the left-hand column and your destination city at the top. Follow the horizontal and vertical rows until you reach the number that corresponds to both. It will tell you the distance between the two cities.

Those who are going to less common destinations, or who are using alternative routes, should consult the scale bar to determine distances. It is important to remember that you probably cannot just measure the distance between the two points to figure out how far you will have to go. This would tell you how far apart the two places are "as the crow flies"—or along a straight path. Unless places are within a few blocks of each other in the same neighborhood, they are not usually connected by a straight road. Instead, roads usually twist and turn to avoid neighborhoods, mountains, or to reach the best place to cross rivers.

Mileage charts can be handy when you want a rough idea of how long your trip will be.

APPROXIMATE MILEAGE BETWEEN SELECTED CITIES

Mileage may vary according to actual route traveled.

	BRADENTON	BROOKSVILLE	CLEARWATER	DAYTONA BEACH	FORT LAUDERDALE	FORT MYERS	FORT PIERCE	GAINESVILLE	JACKSONVILLE	KEY WEST	LAKELAND	LAKE CITY	LEESBURG	MELBOURNE	MIAMI	NAPLES	OCALA	ORLANDO	PANAMA CITY	PENSACOLA	PUNTA GORDA	ST. PETERSBURG	SARASOTA	TALLAHASSEE	TAMPA	TITUSVILLE	WEST PALM BEACH
BRADENTON		83	42	168	209	84	148	164	223	353	61	204	114	158	220	117	129	114	364	458	60	26	13	272	41	153	176
BROOKSVILLE	83		54	109	261	160	169	83	147	415	52	122	42	131	272	194	53	67	288	381	138	63	96	196	45	106	219
CLEARWATER	42	54		160	249	125	167	129	197	395	54	167	97	150	260	159	103	106	327	421	101	19	55	235	22	146	215
DAYTONA BEACH	168	109	160		229	207	133	98	89	405	108	130	67	86	251	241	76	54	331	425	185	159	181	234	139	46	187
FORT LAUDERDALE	209	261	249	229		133	97	312	317	177	210	353	244	144	22	105	276	209	536	630	154	234	201	444	234	183	43
FORT MYERS	84	160	125	207	133		123	230	285	270	109	271	166	170	141	34	195	153	448	541	24	110	71	356	123	192	124
FORT PIERCE	148	169	167	133	97	123		217	221	272	118	258	150	47	118	154	181	114	441	535	121	165	146	349	145	87	54
GAINESVILLE	164	83	129	98	312	230	217		69	474	121	45	69	175	331	264	37	109	236	330	208	143	177	144	128	142	269
JACKSONVILLE	223	147	197	89	317	285	221	69		493	180	60	123	174	338	319	95	134	260	354	263	208	236	163	188	134	274
KEY WEST	353	415	395	405	177	270	272	474	493		363	514	405	319	155	236	436	371	698	792	293	379	341	606	387	359	219
LAKELAND	61	52	54	108	210	109	118	121	180	363		162	60	98	220	143	87	54	339	433	87	52	74	247	32	93	168
LAKE CITY	204	122	167	130	353	271	258	45	60	514	162		109	215	372	305	78	150	202	295	249	181	217	104	167	175	310
LEESBURG	114	42	97	67	244	166	150	69	123	405	60	109		107	262	199	31	41	293	387	143	99	124	201	79	75	202
MELBOURNE	158	131	150	86	144	170	47	175	174	319	98	215	107		165	201	138	67	399	493	168	149	171	307	129	40	101
MIAMI	220	272	260	251	22	141	118	331	338	155	220	372	262	165		107	294	228	555	649	164	245	211	463	245	204	64
NAPLES	117	194	159	241	105	34	154	264	319	236	143	305	199	201	107		229	187	481	575	57	143	105	389	156	226	147
OCALA	129	53	103	76	276	195	181	37	95	436	87	78	31	138	294	229		72	262	356	173	113	142	170	93	105	233
ORLANDO	114	67	106	54	209	153	114	109	134	371	54	150	41	67	228	187	72		334	428	131	105	127	242	85	40	166
PANAMA CITY	364	288	327	331	536	448	441	236	260	698	339	202	293	399	555	481	262	334		103	424	342	377	97	331	367	493
PENSACOLA	458	381	421	425	630	541	535	330	354	792	433	295	387	493	649	575	356	428	103		517	435	471	191	425	461	587
PUNTA GORDA	60	138	101	185	154	24	121	208	263	293	87	249	143	168	164	57	173	131	424	517		86	47	332	100	170	140
ST. PETERSBURG	26	63	19	159	234	110	165	143	208	379	52	181	99	149	245	143	113	105	342	435	86		39	250	20	144	200
SARASOTA	13	96	55	181	201	71	146	177	236	341	74	217	124	171	211	105	142	127	377	471	47	39		285	53	186	174
TALLAHASSEE	272	196	235	234	444	356	349	144	163	606	247	104	201	307	463	389	170	242	97	191	332	250	285		239	275	401
TAMPA	41	45	22	139	234	123	145	128	188	387	32	167	79	129	245	156	93	85	331	425	100	20	53	239		124	193
TITUSVILLE	153	106	146	46	183	192	87	142	134	359	93	175	75	40	204	226	105	40	367	461	170	144	186	275	124		141
WEST PALM BEACH	176	219	215	187	43	124	54	269	274	219	168	310	202	101	64	147	233	166	493	587	140	200	174	401	193	141	

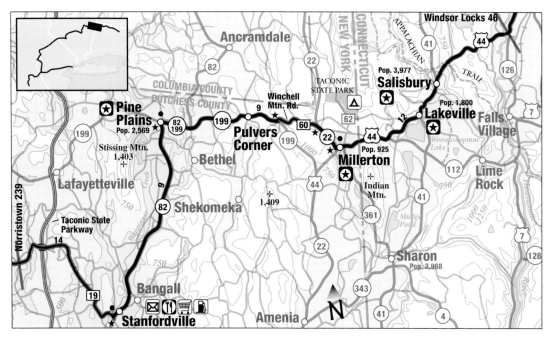

On this map, the black numbers along the routes show how many miles are between each point.

To measure the length of a curvy route, take a piece of string and lay it along the roads you plan to take from your departure point to your destination. Then measure the string to see how long it is. Multiply the length of the route in inches by the number of miles per inch according to the map's scale. The result will be the distance between the two points.

Road maps usually give the number of miles between exits on the highways shown. Look for the tiny numbers beside the lines that indicate the roads.

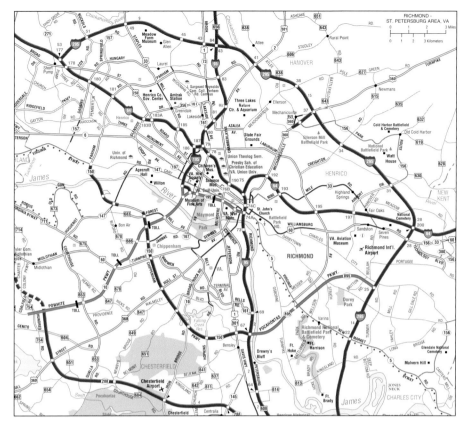

On road maps, thicker lines usually indicate highways or major routes. Thin lines show local roads.

When people have a long way to travel, they usually want to get there as quickly as possible. For that reason, they may plan to take highways—large paved roads with several lanes and high speed limits. Other people prefer to drive on slower roads that let them do some sightseeing as they go. These people choose scenic routes and other roads off the beaten path.

The largest roads in the United States are called freeways or expressways. These are divided highways where cars going different directions are separated by a barrier. Cars can only get on and off of them from special entrances and exits. This way, people can drive for long distances without stopping for things like traffic lights or stop signs. The largest system of expressways in the United States is the interstate highway system. The longest interstates go all the way across the United States, from the East Coast to the West Coast.

Highways are identified by number, and the symbols for them on maps generally match the ones used on road signs. Interstates are indicated by a red, white, and blue shield with a number on it. U.S routes are designated by white shields with numbers. State route symbols differ from state to state, but are often shown by a numbered white oval.

In general, the larger a road is, the thicker the line is to indicate it on the map. If the line is dashed instead of solid, it usually means that the road is under construction. Scenic routes are often marked with a green dotted line. In some states, there are toll roads—roads you have to pay to drive on. They are printed on the map in a special color, too.

Road maps do not have room to show details about the cities on them. But once travelers arrive at their destination, they might need a little help getting around. So road maps usually include **inset maps**, or detail maps, of the cities. These are small maps that give details about part of the main map and are usually at a larger scale. Inset maps can also show areas that do not fit on the main map.

This inset map shows an area that does not fit on the main map.

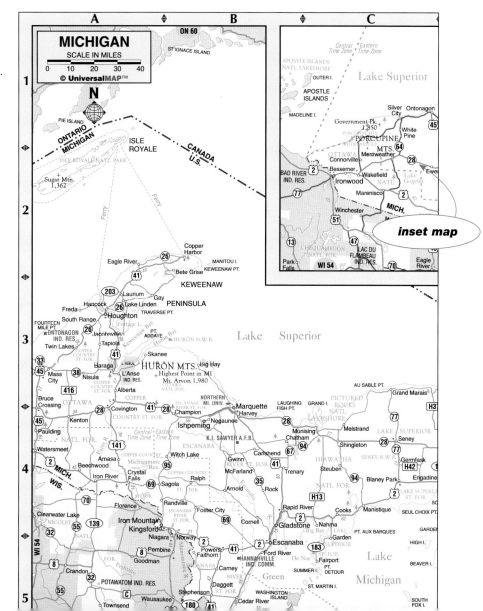

City and Town Maps

To find your way around a city or town, you need a large-scale map with enough detail to show the names of the streets along your route. For many cities, this means you will have several different styles of maps to choose from.

City maps are available on large sheets of paper that are folded up accordion-style just like folded road maps. In addition to the overall picture of the city, they may include inset maps to give you a closer view of popular neighborhoods. You can also find laminated (plastic-coated) folded maps of many cities. These maps generally only focus on the central part of the city. They are great for using while you are walking around outside because they are sturdier than paper, so you can fold and unfold them many times without wearing them out. Plus, your map will be safe if you get caught in the rain. However, if you need lots and lots of details, especially of areas beyond where tourists go, then you will want a street atlas, or collection of larger-scale maps showing every street in the city. Most such atlases have spiral bindings, which make them easy to fold back so you can look at one page at a time.

UniversalMAP

INTERSTATE

Atlas

UNITED STATES · CANADA · MEXICO

where does your map take you?

Totally Updated

Features

Convenient same page city indexes

Inset maps of major cities and metro areas

Extensive points of interest

www.universalmap.com

Some atlases include both large-scale road maps and small-scale city maps.

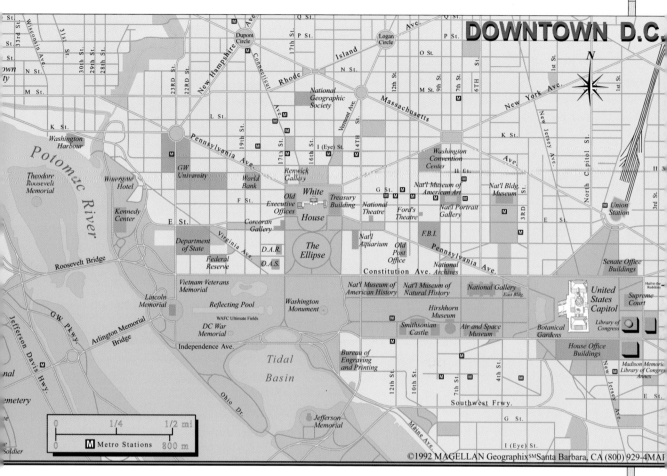

Some city maps do not include a map key. Instead, they label each point of interest right on the map.

   Like road maps, city maps also use symbols, so look to see if your map has a key. City maps are more likely than road maps to include information such as the direction cars can go on one-way streets (look for tiny arrows next to the streets), numbers to help find a house if you know its street name and house number, and places like schools, churches, and shopping centers. City maps that cover the whole metropolitan area (the downtown area and surrounding neighborhoods that make up the city) will give county names and probably even the names of neighborhoods. The index for the map will list all the streets and their location on the grid.

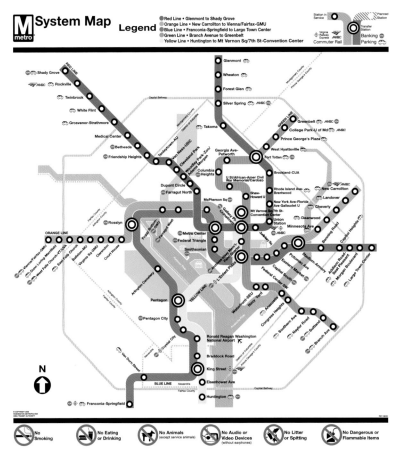

This is a subway map of the Washington, D.C. area. The smaller circles are stops on the train. The larger circles show where you can transfer to another train.

Detailed maps of city streets are useful if you are walking or driving through town, but what if you plan to use public transportation? Buses, subways, and light rail transit systems all have maps that help you figure out how to go from place to place.

When you take public transportation, somebody else does the driving for you, and a schedule determines how long the journey takes. So you do not need most of the information that is found on street maps. What you *do* need to know is which train or bus to catch, where and when to catch it, and where to get off. Most subway and light rail maps show the routes of the trains in different colors, along with the route numbers and all of the stops. They may also show the basic shape of the city. But there will not be many, if any, streets on them, and they probably will not be "drawn to scale," which means they will not show the correct distances between places. Such maps are called **topological maps**—they concentrate on relationships between places, such as the order of stops on a subway line, rather than the exact location of each.

Since buses travel the roads along with cars, bus maps usually look more like street maps, with numbered lines marking the routes. They might also include a timetable that tells when the bus stops at certain points along the route.

The key for a public transportation map can contain important information. For example, it may explain how to tell an express bus (one that only makes a few stops along the route so it can travel faster) from a local bus (one that makes all the stops). Or it may explain the symbol that shows where you can transfer to other subway or bus lines.

You might want to use both a street map and a public transportation map when you plan your trip. Together, these maps will help you find your way around a new place.

Bus maps often use a "T" inside a circle to show where you can transfer to another bus line. Study the map key to find out what the other symbols mean.

Neighborhood and Other Limited-Area Maps

Sometimes even a city map covers too much ground if you are planning to spend your time exploring a small area, like a particular neighborhood. Among the most common neighborhood maps are tourist maps. You can get these for free at city and town information booths and from businesses that serve lots of sightseers. These maps usually do not show the whole city, just the area most people want to spend time in.

Tourist picture maps like this one include a lot of detail, such as the size and shapes of buildings.

Because these large-scale maps have room to include so much detail, there are often pictures on them to make the attractions stand out. Instead of showing just a bird's-eye-view picture from above, they might show a different angle. The buildings could be drawn with enough detail to help you recognize them when you walk up to them in real life. There might be little animals where the zoo is or boats on the lake where you can go sailing. Sometimes an index is not necessary for tourist maps because there is enough room to label everything directly on the map.

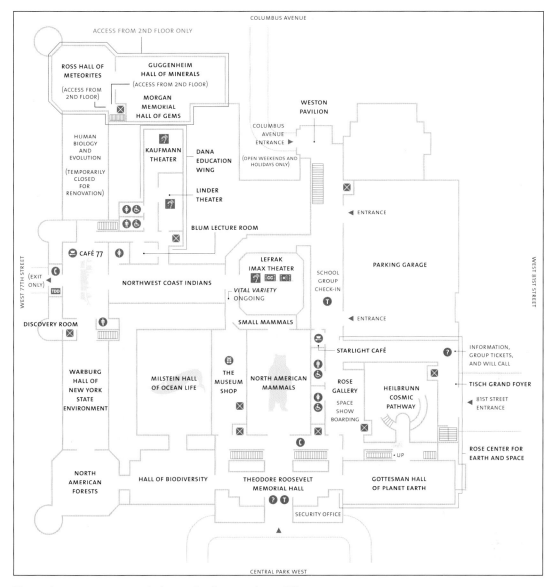

Floor plans may use symbols or shading to show different areas.

Another type of large-scale map that you are likely to encounter is a floor plan or ground plan. You will find these posted near the entrances to places such as museums, zoos, theme parks, or shopping malls. These maps usually consist of an outline of the building that is divided into the different sections or rooms inside. Each area may be labeled with a number or letter, or it may list the name of that area if there is room on the map. These maps also list symbols to help you locate things such as restrooms or information areas.

Sometimes the different areas are color-coded according to type. For example, on the floor plan for a shopping mall, restaurants may be one color, while clothing stores would be another color. These maps sometimes mark the spot where you are located with an arrow and the words "You are here" to help you get your bearings.

Other Maps That Help You Find Your Way

Maps are not just helpful on paved roads. They can guide you when you are out in the wilderness, too. If you visit a national or state park, often a map will be available for free at the park's information booth. Park maps have many of the usual features: a compass rose, scale bar, and map key. They will show the roads leading to and through the park. They will also include all of the park attractions, such as campgrounds, picnic spots, and ranger stations.

Park maps may show hiking trails, but if you are going hiking, you might want to get an even larger-scale map that focuses on a single trail or network of trails. On color maps, the various trails are usually shown in different colors, so you can be sure that you are following the right route by watching for trail markers, or "blazes," that are the same color (look for signs beside the path and painted marks on trees or rocks).

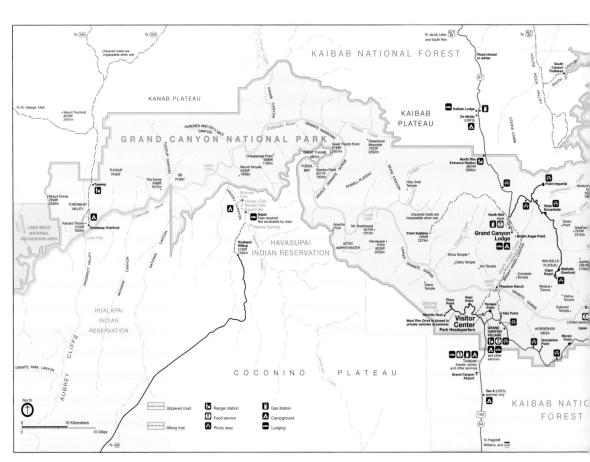

Park maps may show points of interest, along with major roads that run through the area.

Both park maps and hiking maps are likely to be **relief** or **topographic maps**. Relief maps show the lumps and bumps of the land by using light and shadow to create a three-dimensional picture. Topographic maps use contour lines to show the exact elevation of an area. Contour lines connect points that are at the same altitude (height of the land above sea level) and usually look like wavy loops. Lines that are right next to each other are at different heights. If they are close together, they describe a steep angle. If they are far away from one another, they describe a gentle slope.

This map uses different types of lines to show different hiking trails. The brown lines in the background are contour lines.

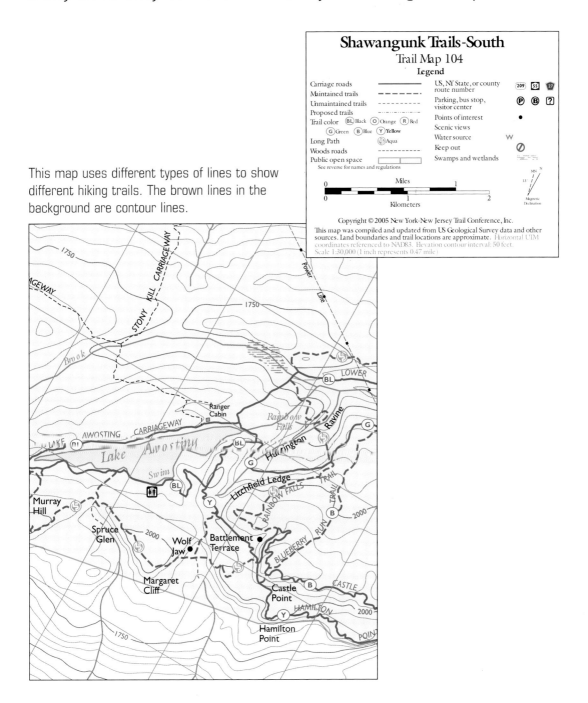

Maps of the Future

It is going to be a long time before maps made of paper go out of fashion since they are so convenient. They fold down into a bundle small enough to carry in your pocket and open up into a big, detailed picture. But the electronic versions of maps are getting better and better. Web sites such as Yahoo! Maps, MapQuest, Google, and Expedia offer free online access to street maps of most places in the world. When you find a map at these sites, you can go from small scale to very large scale by clicking the zoom function and centering in on the detail you are most interested in. For many locations, especially within the United States, these Web sites will even provide driving directions between any two places you request.

zoom
function

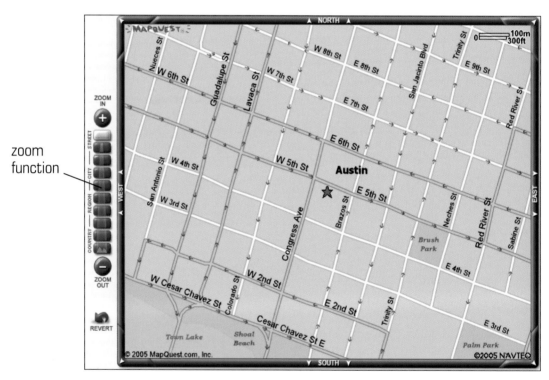

With access to a computer and the Internet, you can easily get a map of almost any location.

Established map companies now sell their atlases on CD-ROMs for computer users who would like to have them available in digital format. But electronic maps require you to either take your computer along when you travel or to print out the maps. Computers do not fit into the glove compartment of a car the way paper maps do, and printouts cannot be any larger than a standard sheet of paper. So for practical reasons, most travelers still prefer traditional maps when they are on the road.

One type of electronic map that is becoming increasingly popular for travelers is the GPS (or Global Positioning System) receiver. This is a device that can communicate with satellites in orbit around the Earth. Gathering information from four or more of these satellites through radio signals, the GPS receiver calculates its latitude, longitude, and altitude. If you are holding the receiver, you know your **absolute location** on Earth! The GPS reader then translates that information and creates a map on its screen. There are small handheld GPS receivers that are designed for carrying around. These can be useful in many situations, such as when you are hiking. There are also larger GPS devices for vehicles. These devices understand voice commands and can translate the positioning information into driving instructions, which the device then says out loud. No need to pull over to the side of the road and open up a map— the GPS system tells you how to get there!

GPS receivers pinpoint your exact location no matter where you are.

Mapping technologies continue to change, but our uses of maps remain the same. Once you learn the basics of how to read a map to find your way, you can embark on many new adventures!

Map Activity: Find Your Way in the Capital City

Here is a map of the nation's capital, Washington, D.C. Imagine that you have a whole day to spend exploring the city. Try finding your way to the locations below. Answers can be found at the bottom of page 29.

1. You begin at the Washington Monument. You decide to go to the White House next. Which direction should you walk?

2. After that, you decide to visit the United States Capitol. Which direction should you walk now?

3. Oh, but what about the Lincoln Memorial? You want to see that. About how far will you have to walk from the Capitol building?

4. Take your time looking at the map—there are a lot of interesting places to visit in Washington. Which ones would you like to see most?

Now that you know about finding your way using maps, you can do all kinds of fun things. Think about trying one of these activities:

- Draw maps of familiar places, like your room, your house, your school, or your neighborhood.

- Hide a treasure and make a treasure map for your friends to follow— mark the spot where the treasure is with an X.

- Sketch out a map the next time somebody asks you for directions.

- Ask for your own map the next time your family goes traveling. See if you can follow the route on the map while you are on the road.

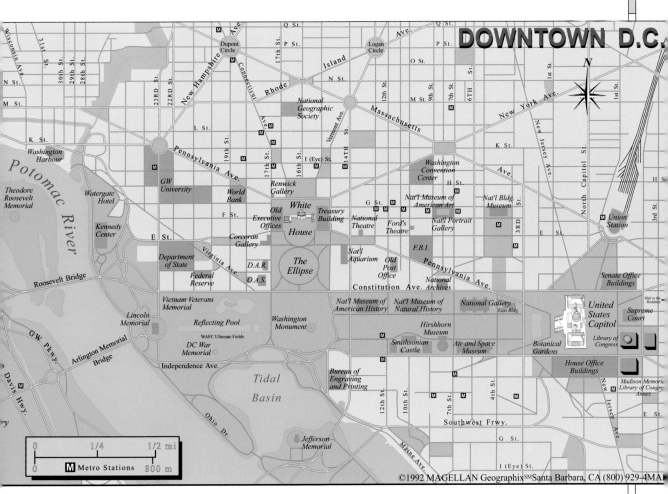

DOWNTOWN D.C.

©1992 MAGELLAN Geographix℠Santa Barbara, CA (800) 929-4MA

Answers to Map Activity

1. North; 2. Southeast—take Pennsylvania Avenue; 3. A little over two and a quarter miles; 4. The answer depends on you!

Glossary

absolute location location of a spot on Earth determined by a standard system, such as latitude and longitude

cardinal direction one of the four main directions including north, south, east, and west

cartographer person who makes maps

compass rose symbol on a map that indicates the cardinal directions

degree unit for measuring distance along the edge of a circle; latitudes and longitudes are marked in degrees

geographic grid system that divides a map into smaller squares using horizontal and vertical lines so you can find places more easily

index list of places shown, along with their location on the map

inset map also called a detail map; a detailed (larger-scale) map of a place within a smaller-scale map; it is either along the edges of the larger map or on the other side of the paper

large-scale map map that shows a fairly small area on which details are relatively large

latitude measure of how far north or south places are on the globe. Latitude lines are imaginary horizontal rings on the globe created by mapmakers to indicate position. Latitude lines are also called parallels.

longitude measure of how far east or west places are on the globe. Longitude lines are imaginary vertical rings on the globe created by mapmakers to indicate position. Longitude lines are also called meridians.

map key also called map legend. A table that shows and explains all symbols, lines, and colors used on a map.

map scale amount that a map has been reduced from the size of the real place

map title feature on a map that identifies the content of the map

mileage distance expressed in miles

mileage table also called mileage chart. A table that shows the distances between cities on a map

relief map map that shows differences in land height with shading

scale bar feature on a map that tells you the relationship between a distance on the map and the distance in the real world

small-scale map map that shows a large area, on which individual details are relatively small

topographic map map that shows differences in land height using contour lines

topological map simplified map, like a bus or subway map, that focuses on the relative location of places. Topological maps are often not drawn to scale.

Further Reading

Blandford, Percy W. *The New Explorer's Guide to Maps and Compasses.* Glencoe, IL: McGraw-Hill School Education Group, 1992.

Bramwell, Martyn. *Maps in Everyday Life.* Minneapolis: Lerner Publications, 1997.

Weiss, Harvey. *Maps: Getting from Here to There.* New York: Houghton Mifflin Company, 1991.

Index

agricultural maps, 4
atlases, 12, 18, *18*

blazes, 24
bus maps, 21, *21*

cardinal directions, 8
cartographers, 6
city maps, 5, *5*, 18, 19, *19*
color-coding, 9, 17, 20, 23, 24
compass rose, 8, 24
contour lines, 25, *25*

degrees, 10
detail maps. *See* inset maps.

electronic maps, 26–27, *26*
expressways, 16

Fisher, Carl Graham, 12
floor plans, 23, *23*
folded maps, 12, 18, 26
freeways, 16

geographic grid, 10, *10*
GPS (or Global Positioning System) receivers, 27, *27*
grid systems, 11, 19
ground plans, 23

highway maps, 5, 16–17
highways, 16
hiking trail maps, 5, *5*, 24–25

indexes, 11, 19, 22
inset maps, 17
interstate highway system, 16

keys, 9, *9*, 12, 19, 21, 24

laminated maps, 18
large-scale maps, 7, *7*, 18, 22, 23, 24
latitude, 10, *10*
light rail maps, 20
longitude, 10, *10*

meridians. *See* longitude.
mileage tables, 14, *14*

neighborhood maps, 5

parallels. *See* latitude.
park maps, 24–25, *24*
population density maps, 4
Prime Meridian, 10
public transportation maps, 20–21, *20*, *21*

relief maps, 25
road construction, 17
road maps, 5, 9, 12–17, *13*

scale bars, 6, 7, 14, 15, 24
small-scale maps, *6*, 7
street maps, 21, 26
subway maps, 20, *20*
symbols, 9, 19, 23

titles, 6
toll roads, 17
topographic maps, 4, 25, *25*
topological maps, 20
tourist maps, 4, 22, *22*
town maps, 5

Web sites, 26

Italicized numbers indicate illustrations, photographs, or maps.